SKIES

NINE
SKIES

Poems by

A. V. Christie

University of Illinois Press

Urbana and Chicago

© 1997 by A. V. Christie
Manufactured in the United States of America

P 6 5 4 3 2

This book is printed on acid-free paper.

Library of Congress Cataloging-in-Publication Data
Christie, A. V. (Ann V.), 1963–
Nine skies : poems / by A. V. Christie.
p.   cm. — (The national poetry series)
ISBN 10: 0-252-06644-8 (pbk. : alk. paper)
ISBN 13: 978-0-252-06644-3
I. Title. II. Series.
PS3553.H729N5 1997
811'.54—dc20 96-45773
CIP

The National Poetry Series

The National Poetry Series was established in 1978 to publish five collections of poetry annually through five participating publishers. The manuscripts are selected by five poets of national reputation. Publication is funded by James A. Michener, The Copernicus Society of America, Edward J. Piszek, The Lannan Foundation, and the Tiny Tiger Foundation.

1996 Competition Winners

Jeanne Marie Beaumont, *Placebo Effects*
  Selected by William Matthews, published by
  W. W. Norton

A. V. Christie, *Nine Skies*
  Selected by Sandra McPherson, published by the
  University of Illinois Press

Jeff Clark, *The Little Door Slides Back*
  Selected by Ray DiPalma, published by
  Sun & Moon Press

Barbara Cully, *The New Intimacy*
  Selected by Carolyn Forché, published by
  Viking/Penguin Press

Mary Leader, *Red Signature*
  Selected by Deborah Digges, published by
  Graywolf Press

Acknowledgments

Some of these poems, or versions thereof, have appeared in the following journals:

The American Scholar: "Liberty Print"
The Boston Review: "Alchemy," "Darwin Crosses the Andes," "Late Swim"
Boulevard: "Brassai's Lovers"
The City Paper: "Motion Study"
Columbia: "Belongings," "Camp Holiday"
Ethos: "Into the Solid Air"
The Indiana Review: "In My Dream," "Legend," "Nine Skies," "Surround"
The Iowa Review: "Coin," "Eye Brooch," "Glyph," "The Formal Garden" (originally titled "Landscape")
The Massachusetts Review: "Passage"
The Plum Review: "Along the Avenue," "Your Harmonica"
Poetry Northwest: "Evermay-on-the-Delaware"
Sonora Review: "Their Titanic"
Southern Poetry Review: "Rumor"

"Late Swim" also appeared in the *1995 / 1996 Anthology of Magazine Verse and Yearbook of American Poetry*

It is a pleasure to thank the Maryland State Arts Council, the Mayor's Advisory Committee on Arts and Culture in Baltimore, and Vassar College's W. K. Rose Fellowship for the Creative Arts for their support and encouragement. And, in particular, my deep appreciation to Elizabeth Spires and to Stuart Christie.

for Andrew
1957–1990

and for John

Contents

I

ANDREW HEARS THE VOICE OF HIS OWN ELEGY

I watch the candle flame, long in the spoon
as the room resounds with all
    that my brothers and sisters do not know.
  They think this meal will bring me back
to them. They ask what would I like
    and pass me bowls, full and steaming.

  All the love-ridden afternoon they gathered in.
Careful pictures were taken.
    As the shutter flicked its pale lid,
  I felt the hand on my shoulder
and looked off over my brother's head,
    his body there like a sorry shield.

  Catching the football, taking each clean spiral
deep in my lungs, I saw them
    wanting it to fall like some heavy joy
  finally come into my life, into my arms.
A sudden flock of birds interrupted
    the last pass into evening.

  Each face turned slowly, wishfully up.
Didn't they hear a wild sound
    chip the faltering sky? Or did the flock
  remind them of a young man writing home
from the Galápagos of feeding Darwin's finches
    green pepper, orange peel and chocolate?

They must have imagined, reading the letter,
air stirred with amber and scarlet.
      But the finches were dull-colored: dun,
    mostly, and black. They didn't eat what I'd cast,
instead scattered with their myriad, famous beaks
    back to the scrub, to the hot, black ground.

I remember now how the air closed in.
How what they don't know will hurt
      soon: they'll dream over and over the .38's
chill zero approaching the very temple lit
now by the candle's flame. I could have killed them—
    they'll know that instead I left them to live

with the finches always in the air behind them.

MOTION STUDY

At dusk in the top bunk your plastic squadrons approached.
With decal snarls, they hung from the ceiling from invisible threads—
dim silhouettes, countless old war movies, the quiet onslaught.

Black Lionel locomotives shone poised on the shelf
—trackless—without the morse of their oily, false smoke.
Your room a secret terminal, the motion beginning.

You studied each constellation stalled on your wall,
the varied wings of your insect collection: moths tidily pinned,
cobalt dragonflies, thoraxes striped like fuses.

Lying on the floor one afternoon, you pulled rubber bands taut,
shot down each swaying model airplane. You perfected the whining
fall and the throaty sound of their exploding.

All through the evenings your wrenches hurriedly rang
the cement; the car rocked on its blocks as you raced the engine.
Legs forked out on the ground like a divining rod

from beneath your Austin-Healey's shining flank,
you completed the apprenticeship,
saw in the sooted heavens how all along you'd been

greasing the gears of your own departure.

BELONGINGS

I put aside the swim team ribbons,
crimped and shimmering, the varsity letters
like thick carpet over your wild heart.

I could string them to your memory, lift you
high on the breeze for everyone to see. It would be easy.
A shaking of heads, words like *shame* or *fine young man*.

They wouldn't know how you clung to a bar
all afternoon, hung there until you couldn't feel your arms,
at Stanley Junior High, a new Iron Man.

No, these honors flash a long tail of hurt in the sun.
Better to use them like shining lures, like junk
that catches the fish's eye, to troll the silence.

In your bottom drawer I find the heavy box of bullets,
spill them, a school of minnows on the rug.
I want your tallest fishing rod.

I want the few glittering feathers left
from your fly tying. How the hooked insects appeared
in your hands, a little thread and there were wings.

And give me the blues harp. You had it a long time.
I smell your cigarettes when I breathe in,
and again in the flat wail of the tune.

We make our own stories
of where these things have been, how very close
or in just what inner pocket you kept them.

I keep the cardboard scrap. On it a quick list
before one of your disappearances: *matches, peanut butter,
hard boiled eggs, cigarettes, twine, matches.*

This can mean what I want—bonfire, plea,
you repeatedly cradling the wan flame in your hands
and standing against the wind.

I reach down to your underwear, limp on the floor;
I take them—a litter of blown flowers—
and throw them away.

PASSAGE

We with love will proudly hoist
those tatters made whole, so tailored for speed.
                                        —Andrew Christie

My hand on your shoulder, I touched the end.
Your legs were drawn in. I saw the rim of underwear
above your pants; your jacket had shifted up, and there
was the taut and hollow spot below your last rib;
full-blown, your head in a bag like I throw my garbage in.
I think I could have withstood seeing whatever hint
of jaw or proud cheek held. And so, on this train,
fleeing from afternoon into evening—in a place
where you never were—you draw near, you begin.
Clouds move off on the wind, the train stirring up a trail
of turning leaves. A man whispers plans for the evening
in his lover's ear. A strand of her hair lifts on his breath.
A woman paints her lips a deep and deeper red.
In overheard conversations I hear more loudly the names
of places where you've been. I look at pictures of the Galápagos
and say to myself, his steps are still somewhere in the rocks,
his handprint still somehow in the whorled shell of the tortoise.
Like the professor—the Thoreauvian—who as a young man
uprooted a sapling from the edge of Walden Pond
and planted it on his own land in Halifax, Vermont. Like him
who lives on in that tree, you intervene in my bones, my joy
will be half yours. We pulled back our hair, cut a lock
from the nape to be burned with you, our necks pale
with January. When Ron Calder, the man who found you
on the playing field, said we didn't have to worry
about your having been out all night, all I could think of

was how cold and quiet it must have been. I imagined rain
pooling in your ear. But he meant that no animals had come
out from the pines to get at you. I see a blur of trees
from the train. They slow: each stop is just where we left it—
Laurel, Savage, St. Denis—I see the school. On the field
cheerleaders are still practicing. Their slender arms
make circles in the air, small angles; their skirts flare
as they jump. I think she was a cheerleader. In shadow,
the two of you shifted and bloomed like underwater things
in your old De Soto, spray-paint clouds down the sides. I try
to remember days at a time, but all is still about you.
You do a chin-up to the bar in the doorway or the splash
before you in the water turns to glass; you look at me
through the tension and pause of your thoughts. You skip
rocks out across the lake while over in the hills above Westbank
the planes leave streams of pink falling toward the fire.
Coming out from beneath your car, you hold a greasy bolt
to the light like a jewel; you sit in the dark, drag hard
on a cigarette, alight in the passing minutes with your own breath.
When I began the journey back to my coast after your death
I watched out over the Cessna's wing as the peninsula receded,
as the waves incessant off Point Roberts changed to a still,
grey blanket. So changed did the world seem to me
that I expected to see out my window row houses caving in
one by one all down my street, like the slow-motion footage
of earthquakes or a city's warehouses wired with explosives,
walls dropping away and the dust rising. I expected disaster,
a turbulent weather, to see just the marble steps left—the climb
to nowhere—trees uprooted, cars blown one atop the other,
their windows a violent Detroit lace. But there was no collapse.
The painters, suspended in their rigging, continued painting.
They whistled in the sun and one warm day, took off their shirts
and their muscles were beautiful, the chiaroscuro of grief

was beautiful. And finally, painstakingly, I made love to my husband
and it was for you, for all that you gave so suddenly away.
The croon of the train spreads into evening, light spills
before it on the track. The baby who wakes to every loud sound
sleeps through the whistle, and the woman's lost keys
have been returned by the conductor who tells her not to worry.
She had wondered how she would make it home. Daylight
is failing in the windows. Standard time: lights in the houses
come on. Maybe somewhere a brother tucks his sister
in a cardboard box with her blanket, pushes her gently
around the house. Maybe the girl pretends it is her coffin
and perhaps the brother, looking at her small hands,
thinks that living is enough. I remember the landscape
of plywood flat on two sawhorses. In the afternoons
under the mulberry, you and a friend set about making a world
for the train. You smoothed plaster over the fretwork
of chicken wire to make mountains; out of your cupped hands:
foothills. Each day further and further along—a resin stream
with flecks of tinfoil fish in it beside the tracks.
There was no city, just open, endowed land
which the train might traverse in ovals and come to know.
With your own hand you could make this world go wild:
whining speeds and grand wrecks on the turns. On the playing field
I put my hand in your blood. I made a handprint with it
on a piece of paper. I did not know what to do. I remembered
the many hands pressed into clay for Mother, your handprints
all over the bathroom, perfect in grease on the mirror, grey
on the soap. Your voice travels further into the distance.
Starting the long journey before us, you cut brush from the trails,
look back over your shoulder. You are like the sunken barge
in the lake. Dangerous, mysterious, we swim above you—
the sun is warm on our arms. We feel you in our bones
swimming over. But we come to shore, brush towels softly

against our necks, wrapped in our stories and myths.
The train eases into Camden Station, where men work
in the floodlights, building the new stadium. Dust they kick up
—caught in the light—makes their silhouettes barely solid.
I walk the platform. To the left: the old, block-long warehouse,
some 300 windows, a few of them bricked in, but always
the one light on in the one at the end. Pigeons wheel up
like newsprint into the rafters of the station: a quivering
sound as I walk home through the life you deepened.
Men gather round trash cans, rub their hands together, bonfire
full on their faces. How it drizzled day and night as the shock
wore off, a small fire snapping in the fireplace. I would walk
to the playing field and then deliberately back:
each step hard on the ground, the steps you did not take
and your dogs would run to meet me, the smell of woodsmoke
deep in their fur. How I used to blot up your wet steps—
brought inside from the lake—so the wood floors wouldn't warp.
And then there was no rain the day of your funeral. The Indians
say when the long rain ceases on such a day, there is no god
wanting to wash your footsteps away. Midnight off San Cristóbal:
you wrote home in the moon's wan light, the unknown stars
presiding. On your night watch you described dolphins
bringing you into harbor, the unmistakable sound of their blowing.
"They appear in an endless, dark water where phosphorescence
is great, trailing white light behind them," you said,
"their paths perfectly parallel and disappearing." The day before
my flight out, I found letters from your voyage, ran my fingers
over the words—passage, tortuga, *Birrahlee,* leeward, music—
felt their grip in the insubstantial paper. Then I came home
into my life, marked by you like the old table where your words
are still: backward, each syllable rough in the soft wood.

YOUR HARMONICA

Their coming back seems possible
For many an ardent year.
　　　　　　　—Emily Dickinson

The words I have spoken since,
the full breath in-drawn to the song,
a want-torn sort of aftercalling—
all part of the air from my lungs.
It croons in the slats, the blues
cupboards—shines, blurs its minor
whine through the slant-lit classroom
and the children making poems
shape its sharp, garish squall
into a candy apple. They raise
their almost translucent hands,
tell me it's like hearing San Francisco;
its brash glissando, the stirring
in a puddle the last rainy day
they remember. They close their eyes
to those darker dramas: the swoon
and blare of sirens
all the dissonant afternoon,
someone falling downstairs.
No, they hear in its warping tune
the last brilliant inch
of the silver-pooling sun going down.
There—behind eyelids, spelling words,
math problems, the imagination trembles
and yearns. The harmonica, flat
and cool now in my hand,

is like a rock you'd skip past
the sunken barge and out toward Penticton,
a barge gone down
through dark legend: sea serpents, horses lost
swimming in from the island.
I hear, then, a deep blue,
just-past-midnight sound
of lights from Westbank mingling
in the water. I, too, picture something
sinking, I tell them. Something
we can't bring back up,
but something intact—like a voice
saying even just one thing we remember.

IN MY DREAM

you live in the thousand rooms
behind the Medusa doorknocker. Verdigris spills
its shock of turquoise through her skull, twists
in the fist-held braids coiling into serpents.
When I knock, you turn more and more to stone.

You tell me the angels are following:
I hear their wings beat in your breath.
Turning your clothes on the line to flame,
you watch ash spiral up, catch in the branches
outside your window. *They were too heavy,* you say.

The moon flashes like a lure, gloves my hands
as I reach past its light to cover you.
The back of your head is gone: your skull a thick frieze
of angels chiseled deeply. You mutter in sleep:
what's rustling, dead pockets, black wings.

All afternoon you strip the oleander of leaves.
Such are the messages received from songs, an overlapping
of strings insisting. You send me the last leaf, enclose
a poem about how my hands, in the moon's white gloves,
settle in your dreams. They are a kind of invitation.

I am holding a mirror in my palm.
The streetlight shines from it into her face
blooming with ruin. She neither leaves
nor speaks. Her bronze lips reveal nothing.
Already it is hard to make your heart move.

Midnight: a hollow sound, your piss
in the toilet too loud through the walls of my room.
I look out over the courtyard. All stone, you stand
in the fountain—the arc of water shining.
I toss my lucky coin and the house falls down.

ACROSTIC FOR MOTHER

That you'd live through a son's funeral, bells loud and
Impossible, one husband gone into
Nevada for good, watch another stand on
The cliffs, the sea off Gualala towering white behind him.
In the weak afternoons of a girlhood pneumonia
Never could you have imagined. You turned quietly from M to
N in the dictionary and read on in bed, learning each word
And some part of its meaning. Never imagining crocuses
Before you, a woman down on her knees watching them come
Up to her, back through the ground, what it might mean
Later. What the one favorite word might come to mean,
A word ringing its many syllables full.
That one day kneeling to your brass rubbing
In the catacombs—the figure like a miracle appearing—from
Outside you'd hear, all through the glare of afternoon, bells like
Nothing from the old days in the Joe Rich Valley.

LIBERTY PRINT

For my sister

Under the abiding lamp, appearances and disappearances;
the needle shines: up through the billow of pale hydrangea,
back down into daphne,
small strawberry blossoms,
beneath the fragile green.

        This fine cotton is tired and thin.
Each time I wear the blouse the strain pulls at the twilit wild rose
and morning glories fray along their immaculate edges.

You brought the Liberty cotton home
from your year at the Sorbonne, folded sharp-cornered
like handkerchiefs in your suitcase, to make each of us a blouse.

You spread the flawless cloth out on the table,
a rustle as you pinned the tissue pattern pieces down.

Yours also floral, warm-hued with slight yellows.

Mine was this fluctuation of lavender, half-sky and green
with a deep blue intruding from the background like a stain,
    an afterthought.

        You told me then as the shears hissed
how one evening in the café you'd tried to ask a man

when the Eiffel Tower's lights might come on. *A quelle heure
la tour s'allume?* you'd said.
        When would it be lit on fire?

This was long before we knew of danger.

The pattern was easy to follow;
the pins shone, a cheerful path into the light.

...

The light shines in the eye of the needle I thread once again
to mend the frail seams ill-worn by a day's reaching.

I begin near the shoulder seam, the dark blue here
                    like a shadow, like midnight.

The lamp illuminates the patient stitches,
loops of purple thread, a collar pressed still
to its precise and thoughtful point.

You were sewing one afternoon—lost in a daydream—
needles and pins sharp from your mouth like a fish's whiskers.
When you swallowed one
                    we made jokes about how for eternity
you'd set off airport security systems.
                    We were afraid.

The doctor never found the needle on the X ray.
At any time it could, like some shimmering pickerel, swim
through you, right to your heart.
        But it disappeared in a cushion of tissue.

This morning you mentioned the calm,
the woman putting one hundred needles in your skin.
        To help the grief, you said.

I imagined the needle stirring in you,
thinking it had come finally into the afterlife,
had rejoined a bristling host of the lost
in the quiet of your flesh.

And I thought what it would be like
                    —you and I, the rest of us—
that moment, seeing again the brother we lost
just a silent year ago.

After we hung up I took out the blouse.
The scissors caught like kindling in the lamplight
                    as I made the first, long cut
toward the first corner of a handkerchief.

IDÉE FIXE

As a child I made the bruise,
ornate, beautiful around my eye,
an afternoon's art, its fluctuate hues
equivalent to a hoarse, thwarted cry.
He once shone the flashlight up
into the suburban sky, my father:
this will go on forever.
He once opened the car door
so I could see the aggregate danger
blur by. And when that light returns
like the bateau mouche's blinding second,
its slowed sweep, I stand so white,
searchlit and still in the awe of testimony.

LATE SWIM

I leave the day behind in the churned light.
The water is sour in my mouth,
each accurate breath new, filled with citronella,
with oleander unfurling its poison in the dark.
            I turn and turn, want to reach you,
want you to dive silently in, rise under me,
clasp my ankle in your hand.
I can almost hear your slick, wet steps
Mother there near the tiki lamp
clipping dead roses heavy into a brown paper bag.

I turn toward the lamplight, swim
into the stutter and shine of home movies
where you paint your white way down a fence.
I hold still your smiling.
            You are lost in a flood of boys
down the steps of your first communion.
Strangely absent in the next frames, just your trout
arranged on the sand, jeweled and diminishing.

The dancers' kilts sway too quickly.
Under a tired sky they dance the sword dance,
            the fling, to your soundless piping.
Near Rushmore you turn to the camera.
I reverse the film: you back away
from the shadowed men, leap
from the aquamarine to the diving board:
the splash healed, I rescue you every time.

SPIRIT LINE

> *. . . whatever has happened lies*
> *beyond our grasp, deep down, deeper than*
> *man can fathom.*
>
> —Ecclesiastes 7:24

Here the nighthawk's silhouette slurs and lilts
against a chalky twilight,
                above the one-after-another
tilt of row houses downtown.
                      At first
I thought he'd lost his mate, so fixed
was his circling and calling out over the same spot.
Everyday the telltale plummeting.

        What was it in the plains you saw ruined?
the buffalo's slow drift across the land,
its inevitable shadow
                one and the same as what
had its claim on you.

        What was it you reached for,
then, in the blackberry bush, leaning
from the ladder your whole body in,
your hands stained like someone wanting
                    to live.

When we laid you down, the eagle spread its wings.

Lifting above the cliffs,
                it cocked its white head
from some Indian legend where the eagle has the truth
—face to face with the sun but never blinking—
and a smaller flock of birds banked on the air and fled.

On the wind
there is always, isn't there, the eagle-bone whistle,
its skirling and untranslatable message?

It sends your brother to a butte above the Snake River.
Or there he stands
in the cool, uneven, already interpreted
shadow at Devil's Tower.

You see,
even now, still, we are working this
into some elaborate design with little to go from.

We dye the wool wet with blackberry,
and watch as the nighthawk pulls its weft of cirrus through
to a selvage taut with feathers.

Trees, window frames,
the beams of our ceilings, the looms we are at work on,
looking up into the night's thick motif
    wondering where it is,
if there can be a place for your laughter.

And there is your younger brother
under the slow crab that moves ever sideways
            through the black cancer sky,
memorizing the Snake River's starlit shape as it
meanders through the heartland.

He will bring home the pale warp of it.

It will be our spirit line,
like the weavers of Two Gray Hills worked in:
        a sure path out to the border, an escape
from the middle of the hypnotic design.

for Stuart and his brother

II

COIN

In the dark inside my skull rests a coin—
passage to the next world. The ferryman will take it
from under my tongue. As it warms in his palm
he will mint my body a rich future.

What hidden currency will help in this world?
To whom do I give the ruby-throated birds, breast-bound
and frenzied? my dreams lined with glittering Orion?
the answering song through the flute of bone?

I gather the snow's loose change to give someone.
I save air turned to coins in the frozen pond;
I save the pale moon where, in winter,
geese and swans fold their wings and shine.

ALONG THE AVENUE

I am moving behind a façade of days down the week's long, long street
through hours no one knows are there and places in songs where
the notes line up like tumblers in some combination unlocking desire.
I have chalk on my hands and students politely listen about verbs,
particulars, nouns. If we could only write, I say, about the silver harmonica,
about the rotting Bartletts steaming with bees he made you gather
in brown paper bags. Give that to the reader. They nod, do not see me
in all my particulars, my handprint blatant on the front wall as I think
how a glance, the fateful slant of an afternoon with a future in it,
or origami delicate on a ledge as we spoke through glass turn—
as though on the stroke of midnight—so easily into the clichés
of betrayal and living. Who would know this is the season
when she tied her shoe and ran off into the hills for the last time,
the season for stuttering and repeated scenes, for the signed name,
the gunshot going off—the gunshot as the firmament of starlings startles up,
when the promise of the wedding kiss is put away like some hat
in a storefront replaced with the latest brim, feather or tuft of gaudy satin,
when I come open like an autumn pomegranate from the corner market's
produce stand to the packed galaxy bleeding, all of that ruby-colored
and sweet hurt, the cramped fruit of the concentrated past. And if I begin
to tell you some, beware—for it can keep you here. I may never let you
back into the light. I will want your company under the awning, will want
to be able to say when you ask *What can I do?* anything besides nothing.
And calling and calling for our drinks, the bistro will only have been
a beaded curtain, some elaborate stage set. Thirsty, and in the half-dark
of a little tailor shop I may ask him to dress you up to some perfection

long before any of this happened. While he works at the proper crease,
the break, I will take my brief stroll for air leading around the corner
and into spring when you will be gone back to another neighborhood.
In the shadows thrown down along the sidewalk, meanders
of schoolchildren glide past feeding the last corner of their sandwich
from a pocket to the pigeons. Sudden fire-opal wings bringing back
a clatter of mistakes blurred with the newspaper's flap at the newsstand.
The tabloids say they've got photographs: proof of the underside
of heaven. I turn my pockets inside out, tie three knots in a string
through months spooling under the hunger moon. I walk the alley
below the ballet school, past the child kneeling on pavement
throwing her cold jacks close like a den of spiders or one at a time
far-flung, constellate. Above her in huge squares of light, girls waft
over chalk flowers drawn loosely on the floor. I walk the earth tilted
its odd degree. In my room at the Shangri-la, I'll lie down into a dream:
a dream of crows decorative in the wires, in the blown-clean trees.
Dream until the flamingo-pink neon throbs out and certain of the letters
are gone. I will turn my face upward as if into some lush-hued Renaissance
scene and you will remember me, my heart underground, holding
these months in my hands, the slow hours like a taste in my mouth.
You'll see the curve of my back like the tie in music: the held sound
a long way down through the measures.

SURROUND

In from the humid noon, matinees are fluttering
a cheap indulgence in the dark. Light sweeps
over water out near the buoy and they are calling,
calling his name, the idiot brother who has drowned.
And far out in the bay the Portuguese fishermen
bring him up in their nets; water eases from his mouth
something he doesn't have the words for
as he comes to, afraid of the fish
like a vast and shifting coat of armor around him.
The boatbuilder father who'd bargained his life for this
smooths the noose tight to his neck, steps from the scaffolding
beneath which rose ships. His death, too, prevented,
brought short by a tangled fate of fortunate rope hung from deep
in the high shadows. Suspended there, the ghost
of his own father speaks with him.

After intermission, another pattern of thin shadow
ghosting the screen. Now the grandmother is dying.
She escapes the hospital in snow, bound for an estate
miles out in the country. All there is of her is this destination.
When the family finds her, they light fires
in all the stone fireplaces until the house is warm.
A young man, a friend of the family, finds her satin shoes
put away in the crook of a tree the lengths of how many
summers ago. He places them, pauses with them in her hands
like a fruit just ripened. She mistakes him for her husband.

The metaphor for dying is long and beautiful.
As though she were moving through rooms of the estate,
closing up the place. In a fur hat and wrap,
she prepares to go, pulls the heavy curtains to:
a phoenix brocade from right and left.
She closes the door behind her.

        A few days later visiting her grave, a clutch of roses
vivid, colorized against the slow white of Montreal,
he sees a woman standing before the elaborate crypt,
its urns and columns looking sculpted from snow.
Her face is upward to the light. So like a movie star
and all in fur. She thinks she knows him,
parts with just the cold-held breath of a kiss.

And this is how it is. Everywhere ghosts walk
from their mirrors; every day those who narrowly escape death
and it becomes a story they tell, rich with props
and redemption. I almost believe you might come.
I plan my return to the blackberry bush, my climb
into the hills of Buckeye Ranch, hawks precise in their circling.

The tree is in full leaf beneath which the birds are buried
in an ever-flickering shade. Dying like harbingers
in the weeks before your death, one of them in my hands—
he weighed about the same as the few bills and change
it took to bring him home. A shudder and then
there never was a body so empty, I thought.
And just now coming out into the thunder and heft of summer,
I catch in the air the press of rain. How would I know
if you were coming? Would there be something tangible
in the stillness? Have you already been and I
have not been looking, listening deeply enough?

All afternoon I listen to my canary, the color
of tangerines. He knows everything that the light intends,
knows the prescient fluctuations of the morning, hears
the shadows lengthen. As I wash dishes, he tunes his song
to the pots and pans, to water, its scale up the cup:
a clear tone calling for accompaniment. He sings and sings
to what I see through, to what I can barely hear.

SOMEWHERE PAST FLESH

Those '70s lyrics, souvenirs of the air
they last in: insubstantial, yet a kind of forever.
Their few minutes tune a half-life in the blood.
In Rodin's sketches Rilke saw hands
he knew would "rest for centuries at the edge
of a lap." Oh, the unaffected curve
of the paper clip in the corner of a dark box
in my basement, or the vaccine's rim
on the pale underside of my arm lasting
like footsteps on the moon
or the too ancient dog of Pompeii, so white
and solid in the ash that claimed him.
The nurserymen concoct the elusive
black rose for their life lists: it will persevere
like whiskey sours or Murderer's Row
or nuclear shadow. And that trill in that measure
will waver through years. Pressed somewhere
past *flesh,* a few leaves from the linden—
how is it in between pages, each summer's
sweet and fugitive air. How can there
be no place for you here in this poem?

INTO THE SOLID AIR

Ice fogs over water like cataracts,
casts shadows which join and dim.
Ascending into the solid air, three whales ram
the closed sky, heads covered in barnacles,
scarred with each attempt.

Do they remember the ease
of heaving those bodies into sunlight?

Caught in the one lit column,
in the trap of their breath, they rise
like belief to unleash skyward
a flawed and necessary mist.

They continue to search.
Where are the bounds of darkness?
Airless and far off that place
to cross into light.

Each night the news transports us
to that hem of ice
where, as winter seals them in,
something in us is opening long enough
for the pure struggle to be seen.

"SEATED GIRL WITH DOG"

Milton Avery

Only half herself,
she holds a dog without shape in her lap.

She does not look out the window
on orange fire escapes knifed in paint:

the faint chute-and-ladder pattern
just a childhood behind her.

Would Avery have us think
what divides her is shadow?

Her lilac block of blouse (half plum),
her hair—blonde parted into brown—

her blank, eclipsed face
are a window's games of light?

No, she lets darkness steal across her,
feeds it bright colors of youth.

Soon she will be all shadow, a woman
with nothing to hold, the dog

just a dark fold between her legs.

THEIR TITANIC

for Zoe

In a dark theater, children startle at the stereophonic sound
of pressure, at the pale green water bubbling up
around them, at the sudden descent.
Could be the beginning of some bad dream
they can't put a finger on, pulling into night's
harbor all their lives long. The ocean goes dim
just as the lights filing in to this
large format field trip. So real we are reeling
back in time on the White Star Line, the insignia
a small flag, a twist of ribbon worn in the hair.
Back to the draft horses dragging the anchor
through the streets of Belfast, way back
into legend, a boatbuilder riveted into the hull.
We hear him calling, iceberg ice singing
in cocktails as the ship goes down. Isn't this almost
the size of our fear, eleven stories, that vast man-made
thing? The searchlight pauses on a banister
with a lyre design, on a stack of plates,
some upright tea cups skittering along like wan crabs
and then, all through the auditorium you hear them
recognize it: *Look, a shoe, It's a shoe, There's*
a woman's shoe, A shoe, A shoe, A shoe . . .
And in this exhaled apprehending, an ending.
They understand. The ocean they were pretending
was an untidy room it was now time to clean,
admits to the dark historic, the catastrophic
and, as their teachers have often reminded them,

this planet we all spin so slowly on is mostly ocean.
Now as they ride the bus home afternoons, the shadows
of clouds are terrifying, like a giant hand reaching for them.

LEGEND

Veuillez me montrer sur cette carte.

At a small table in the airport lounge, we held your money to the broad glare from those observation deck windows, held it against the Boeing's shadows, the comings and goings. We saw all the barely-there faces dim and changing hands. And didn't they become, weren't they the ghosts we carry into the wide world, the one maybe watching as we move on? You'd spend your first few weeks in France lighting candles for him: a guttering, minute light to lick the ancient dark of cathedrals. How the slender and pointed flame might look like the first letter of his name there alone on your knees to this rapt pilgrimage. And I'd read how Chartres, late in the twelfth century, burned and burned. For three days, the leaden roof poured down onto the paving stones. I was glad when you slipped their half-glances from beyond the counterfeit back in your large wallet and unfolded the map instead like a paper airplane. "Right here—across from the university," you said and we looked for a place for you to swim in that quarter. I spoke the word *centime . . . centime*, rubbing at the satisfying profile with my thumb. If you couldn't think of the term for laundromat, your clothes might never get clean—or so it seemed. All autumn, I waited for him at Drew's Laundry, Andrew's Wash & Dry as though he'd come for his name, transparent on the window, faint on the wall outside. I readied a trance of whites and delicates turning over and over on themselves so he would step through the door, light going awry. And I swam, the black-tile line trailing behind, like a jet's silent tracing on the sky, for weeks what I'd seen—the sky's abiding feature—looking upward this time, that time. Or maybe I followed the shadow of the water's own remembering, the shadow of what the moon once put down on its surface. Breath after breath, the outer world loud like a waterfall, the clock sweeping round as the list of recordholders changed. And I knew you were also swimming, trying to put some distance in the water behind you. Before you left, we'd gone to the topiary gardens, each point of interest prim and as neatly marked out as the arrondissements: the Keyhole, Water Lily and Berry Gardens. Here the particular iris—even a scheme in the Wild Garden leading us past the yew swans along the undulant hedge and into the plain solemnity of the Great Bowl, right to the destined edge of the oval pool. That night we listened in the dark to rain, something you'd not heard in a long time; the electric storm never came as close as we wanted. Not long after you'd gone, our childhood, oak-gnarled hills burned down to ash and the heady scent of eucalyptus. Even now helicopters drop poppy and wildflower seed, great arcs of it into the charred wind and the thread-like roots of these slight flowers will begin holding the hills together as you sit quietly at the Tuileries, at the prow of Paris's own emblematic galleon—ghosts in your pockets and carrying on.

DARWIN CROSSES THE ANDES

All day we followed the *madrina* up into the mountains,
the steady rise and fall of her flecked, grey flanks tedious and hypnotic.
    The bell around her neck made a modest sound as each hoof
struck the terraced rock, our ten mules following
    their godmother, their long ears flickering to hear her.

During the ascent I felt in my chest the onset of the *puna,*
some small difficulty of breath. Many in Chile do not comprehend this.
    They think it is something in the rock, in the snow,
a power the mountains have. Truths will have their different origins.
    "These waters have *puna,*" they say.

After the stubborn potatoes which would not cook
in the boil of this diminished atmosphere, "in the pot's iron curse,"
    I yearn to reach Mendoza where I hear watermelons are large
as a mule's head and a heaping wheelbarrow's worth
    of peaches, olives or figs can be had for threepence.

Climbing, I've collected thirteen species of mice.
What force is ever-tinkering with such variation?
    What is responsible for each splendid form, the lapses into ruin,
for the wild and profound? for the muddied torrents
    through these mountains, their furious inclination?

Tonight round stones borne end over end along the Maypu
make a hollow underwater sound, haunting above the roar
    toward the ocean. I hear in them time passing irrecoverably by.
My companions sleep through as sparks from the dry wood lift, torrents
    of brilliant lepidoptera in an extravagant sky.

III

*How then does light
return to the world after
the eclipse of the sun?
Miraculously. Frailly.
In thin stripes. It hangs
like a glass cage.*

—Virginia Woolf

EVERMAY-ON-THE-DELAWARE

You sleep in the sharp Adirondack chair,
surrounded by a still cloud of larkspur
and I am in the long shadows of lupine
which almost reach you in late afternoon.
I'm remembering the night of our wedding,
how rain throbbed on the windshield, each drop
a shadow blooming somewhere on the map.
I wanted you to know the way along
roads blurred by a fury of rain. I yearned
for you to reinvent yourself as lightning
spread its repertoire, its variations.
But love is each repetition, each small return;
night after night love is the way you gather
the birds, lifting their cage like a lantern.

BIRD SONG

I am aware
of your swift, allotted heartbeat
    as you shift in water
        you used to flutter
    to a jeweled noise in the saucer,
our reflecting pool on the sill.

Close to the finish, what's done,
a last carmine thread knotted
    in the embroiderer's hand,
        a last stitch into satin
    and you will be part of the implied
in a reduction of grey sky

I see beyond the façade
of a condemned building, beyond
    pediments, garlands, balconies,
        their wrought-iron geometry
    encasing the air; part of the slurried
shadow, the mirage of carp

in the pond; or the few chairs
haphazard and empty in the shade
    there. You will be
        what the old man calls for
    at Sacré-Coeur, holding up my hand
to birds and more than birds.

LANDSCAPE

Eye Brooch

The artisan fashions first the gold rims
of eyes hammered, narrowed to almonds, trims them,
thinks of what cluster of aquamarine,
emerald, pearl, tortoiseshell could suggest
the vast, refracted, heart-thirst of lust best
until they look on one another again.
How to craft all that such a want entails,
some discreet resemblance worn on her breast
or held, gazed on by a mistress until
she almost makes something of the heaviness.
What the encrusted eye cannot replicate,
nor the lover, is that something lost.
Deep, elsewhere, completely without shape—
desire just the chaos of its facets.

Glyph

With each moment we make a history
between us out of secrets, the wet rings
bottles leave on dark tables receding
down the time line, the harbor's blank light,
the Elvis pocketknife in the junk store
where I shook a snowglobe full of glitter
falling on some misremembered landmark.
My legs touching yours, the shared bottle might
be the place to begin deciphering—
with the locusts in the suburban elms,
their long sound as though devouring the night.
And sure, make the bottle make a sound too,
wind in its mouth: deep, anticipatory,
like a foghorn, sustained, a code, a warning.

Camp Holiday

I watch you put the children beneath the dark
of their cardboard boxes; in a small pinhole of light
they think they might see the sun going away.
At night the words come at me
like wayward feathers from a poultry truck
I followed all through the valley—spinning
into air. Words, the right words to say
to slake the something you want, to whet
the inarticulate. Wouldn't we like to put the children
on their amber buses home and then walk across
the shade where squirrels rest then continue on
like script. And we would walk to the railroad tracks,
walk beyond, and right out of our lives—leaving
the net swaying, new words sweet on our tongues.

Brassai's Lovers

stall in moments of welcome and / or farewell,
who can tell on the rue de Lappe, on a bench
in the Tuileries or as they kiss
on a swan boat that swings upward or down?
In the café we see them all angles
a melodrama of dark lipstick, touching
in mirrors on the wall, the sugar cube small
and simple like the shine the teapot leaves
on the table. In the gardens, she disappears
in him, in a dark kiss. It is the lit slats
of the bench, the chestnut trees like chandeliers,
their cascade of flowers that glow, the lovers
not mattering—so sordid, unkempt, precarious
near the perfect curve of the swan's long, gilded neck.

The Formal Garden

We are at the gardens near those stone lions,
rings dangling from their mouths.
The sky is an averaging of greys
and Japanese maples no longer splay
their embellished shadows to lie down in.
Even the sundial is hesitant now.
What time is it, we are wondering
when peonies bow down in their tangles,
when the inspiring press of cardinals
never issued from the birdhouse's black
recess: joyous, in endless sexual.
Surrounded now by a landscape of fact,
how long are we past the hour for turning home,
sprays of forsythia half-lit in our arms?

California Self-Portrait

In January, a milky cuff of ice,
aftermath along the Gunpowder's bank
thousands of miles from this grove of bay trees
near Pt. Reyes where the sun's only half-sure
of its beginning again through the fog.
Back in a schoolroom in the projects
you take down soft construction paper leaves
too long in the windows, stop to notice
how the sun's changed them. I am reaching up
through the air's perfume, through half-silver
whispering for something to keep. I strip
the lower branches, my shirt held so:
like a net, heavy with each thin want,
the shifting periphery of the heart.

RUMOR

for J.M.

I look out past the cramped tables, the predictable
blue and white for the reunion
                  —out to the oaks
where paper lanterns waver, rich
and suggestive in the dark.

I've been waiting for you
               quietly from behind
to touch my shoulder
and for that moment of turning
to see you there.

           I think my breath would go away.

I am afraid of how the want might show:
    some kind of shadow, something going wide
and dark in me
          that you would see.

Looking for you in the gather, the mingle,
the drift through the night of bodies,
I imagine this danger.

            As she sits down
I've just finished scanning the broad lawn,
        those figures drawn close, tinted
wonderfully by the lanterns.

I don't hear what they say to one another
just an accumulation of sound,
                    ice cubes
seductively striking glass in their hands.

I remember her now.
We sang second soprano in the choir.
Here, she seems to know everyone.

She begins whispering about men in love with men.
Behind her hand the breath of rumor is warm

                    —and then your name.

And I can almost feel the still afternoon
my shirt still half-on
                    as you eased away,
dropped your head down and looked for the rest of the song
at me, looked as we heard it how many times

until there was no light left in the room.

I remember the neutral slides into the night,
the many returns home before dawn, parents sleeping
                    through the unknown,

remember etching our names on a fire escape
near the top of the St. Francis, the fog coming in
                    slow over Yerba Buena Island.

I have dreamed us up ladders of fire,
our mouths wet: some raw, mysterious escape—
have dreamed you through too many doorways.

                    Always
your fingers brush at some pulse—wrist or neck—
and we are gone into it.

And because you and my husband share the same name,
I do not know who it is calling.

Over and over in my mind,
        I've come to this forbidden room, this place
far from where I am living.

I've seen the torn shirt, your body
hinting through it, the flicker of muscle up your arm
as you press garlic into a pot of steam,
            the lit wine in our glasses shifting.

And I have wanted you dreaming all along
the length of where our bodies met, that warmth
where mine stopped and yours began,

have wanted to think you still return
            to the balcony,
and, putting your hand across the names,
see me dark but know who I am.

It is me
with all the years spread out behind.
It is me leaning out above the Bay,
        out toward something.

And as she spoke your name just then
I thought out beyond rumor, and watched
my body cease in your dreams.

It could have been
        that my body was like a pale light
coming toward you, a pale light

that went out in a room where,
before lovemaking, I remember you
touching men's cologne to my temple,
            all down my spine.

ALCHEMY

My body goes before me, like a lantern down a dark lane,
bringing one thing after another out of darkness into a ring
of light. . . . My imagination is the body's.

—Virginia Woolf

In the dark morning you leave your empty cup on the counter
and after you've left for work I fill it again to continue.
I watch the milk swirl like a storm (although you take it black).
It is part of my same apprehending, the sound
of cardinals reminding me, long past a hesitant dawn,
just what world I've wakened to. And when I spend up until noon
in your heavy robe, use your toothbrush and pen and then pull
your turtleneck on, is it you I am trying to become?

I could turn to anything: laurel tree, reverberation, rain of coins,
swan . . . But I am more like the swans of Lohengrin, in Boston,
Lowell's swans, all wheel and pedal to move me
when someone sits down—a crude machinery. I have a friend
who wishes she had no body. How she could keep to herself.
A disappearance into pure mind: out beyond shadow, each touch,
each weightless wrong an irrelevance out past the dangerous.
Neither the drift nor pull, no going down on your knees.

And here I am busy with hiding, leaning my thigh to the radiator's
hot rungs, one version of a desire to have done with the body,
this grievance. The shadow of my breast no longer fine
but a place, you think, where my doubts rest and multiply;
and watch what used to be the simple path of your breathy promise
across the nape of my neck, how it catches in the swirl of hair there,
to you like some destructive curl on the weather map, replaying—
over then over—the shift of a certain vengefulness.

My body just some chart now of our impositions—an endless
navigation—or some diagram in a cookbook locating the prime
spots, the outline of the creature a convenience. And when models
in the magazines turn sideways and disappear, I am haunted
by the idea of that, the daydreamed after slick and glossy-aired,
paper-thin elision. If only to be clean for a single moment, something
pure and entire for you in a perfection of my own absence
like the calculated and empty gardens of Villandry

a precision along the Loire, its chalk banks giving off the stretch
of a day's heat into midnight. A still geometry, in relief some neat story
of desire. There a topiary maze of fans, hearts, masks, daggers.
Love's trimmed inconstancy. In the saccadic blur of this panorama,
this tidy cloister, the pulse and frill of ornamental cabbage:
on the perimeter a strewn lace of underthings. Swans moving
smoothly in the moats as though pulled on a string. There along
the angled design of a boxwood salon of pens and love letters.

No, I'll take the flawed clamor of the body, its wanting.
Like some letter written with lemon—the wavering flame will always give
me away, written all up and down. As night opens to its bewilderment
of heliotrope and rosemary, what is better than holding
the sweating glass to the temple, a slight lilt of chimes, the moon
turning my arm pale as a doll's arm, knowing what it is to be
out of breath, the water squeezed from the sponge at the collarbone,
the smell of the sun on you, knowing all of these exquisite threats.

NINE SKIES

In the week when Tsao Wang who hangs
at the stove—the Kitchen God—leaves
for heaven to meet the Jade Emperor
he will speak well of us
for I have wet his lips each morning
with honey. His words will be sweet
as the litchi and he will have forgotten
our weekly misdeeds from the wine
I painted his lips with at night.

We will take him out and burn him
with the paper ladder I cut for his climb.
And we will watch him rise with our fortune
toward a new year, a pale smoke
I'll watch into sky—rising above
our backyard, over the bridge of magpies,
over the man across the street who kneels
painting characters, black and gold
good luck onto narrow banners.

I have already made the ladder,
cutting big squares from the paper—one
blowing out the window like a letter
sent far off. Right after I put the scissors

safe away in the drawer
where we will keep knives
on the long eve of New Year
so there will be nothing sharp
to cut away the good that might come.

We will pull at the chicken, the fish
kept whole to remind us of completeness,
of how two lives come together.
We will savor the fancy mushrooms
each of them like an opportunity.
And there will still be places at the table
set for those who have died, their chopsticks
perfectly parallel—their eight treasures pudding
sitting there before a vast quiet

of misfortune and the luck which took them.
Do not be sad in the year's first moments
you will say in the dark before bed.
I will take my luck money out
from the red envelope, walk careful
through the newness, the poised year.
And above the yard the last smoke
will dissolve like rice candy, or crickets—
a sound gone into the wind.

A. V. Christie was born in 1963 in Redwood City, California, and grew up in nearby Lafayette, spending summers in British Columbia and later in the Pacific Northwest. She is a graduate of Vassar College and of the University of Maryland's MFA program. In 1991, she was selected by Stanley Kunitz as an Academy of American Poets Prizewinner. Her chapbook, *Black and Blues,* was published in 1985. Her poems also have appeared in *Poetry Northwest, The Indiana Review, The Iowa Review, The Massachusetts Review,* and in other journals. She has received grants from the Maryland State Arts Council and the city of Baltimore, where she lives, teaches at Goucher College, and is a Poet-in-the-Schools.

Illinois Poetry Series

LAURENCE LIEBERMAN, EDITOR

Off-Season at the Edge of the World
  Debora Greger (1994)
Counting the Black Angels
  Len Roberts (1994)
Oblivion
  Stephen Berg (1995)
To Us, All Flowers Are Roses
  Lorna Goodison (1995)
Honorable Amendments
  Michael S. Harper (1995)
Points of Departure
  Miller Williams (1995)
Dance Script with Electric Ballerina
  Alice Fulton (reissue, 1996)

To the Bone: New and Selected Poems
  Sydney Lea (1996)
Floating on Solitude
  Dave Smith (3-volume reissue, 1996)
Bruised Paradise
  Kevin Stein (1996)
Walt Whitman Bathing
  David Wagoner (1996)
Rough Cut
  Thomas Swiss (1997)
Paris
  Jim Barnes (1997)

National Poetry Series

Eroding Witness
  Nathaniel Mackey (1985)
  Selected by Michael S. Harper
Palladium
  Alice Fulton (1986)
  Selected by Mark Strand
Cities in Motion
  Sylvia Moss (1987)
  Selected by Derek Walcott
The Hand of God and a Few Bright
  Flowers
  William Olsen (1988)
  Selected by David Wagoner
The Great Bird of Love
  Paul Zimmer (1989)
  Selected by William Stafford
Stubborn
  Roland Flint (1990)
  Selected by Dave Smith
The Surface
  Laura Mullen (1991)
  Selected by C. K. Williams

The Dig
  Lynn Emanuel (1992)
  Selected by Gerald Stern
My Alexandria
  Mark Doty (1993)
  Selected by Philip Levine
The High Road to Taos
  Martin Edmunds (1994)
  Selected by Donald Hall
Theater of Animals
  Samn Stockwell (1995)
  Selected by Louise Glück
The Broken World
  Marcus Cafagña (1996)
  Selected by Yusef Komunyakaa
Nine Skies
  A. V. Christie (1997)
  Selected by Sandra McPherson